Make Two Crocodiles

by Anne Giulieri
photography by Sylvia Kreinberg

Make a Crocodile Card

You can make a *crocodile card* from green card.

Here is the green card.

Here are the *scissors*.

Here is a black *pencil*.

To make your crocodile card, **fold** the paper like this.

Then **draw** a crocodile
on the card like this.
It will have a long *nose*,
two *legs* and a *tail*.

Cut out your crocodile.

Make 6 cuts
on your crocodile's back
like this.

Make your crocodile
like this.

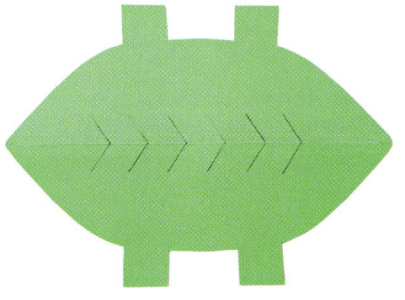

Make *triangles* like this.
The cuts go up.

Cut a *mouth* in your crocodile.

Cut out the *teeth*, too.

Then **draw** two black *eyes* on your crocodile.

This is my crocodile card.

Make a Peg Crocodile

Here is a *peg* for the crocodile.

Here is the *paint* and here is the *brush*.

Here is a *pipe cleaner* for the crocodile's legs.

Here are two eyes for the crocodile.

Here is the *glue* and here are the scissors.

Paint the peg green like this.

Cut the pipe cleaner in two like this.

Bend the pipe cleaners to make the crocodile legs.

The legs go into the peg like this.

The eyes go on
the crocodile like this.

This is my peg crocodile.
Snap! Snap! Snap!

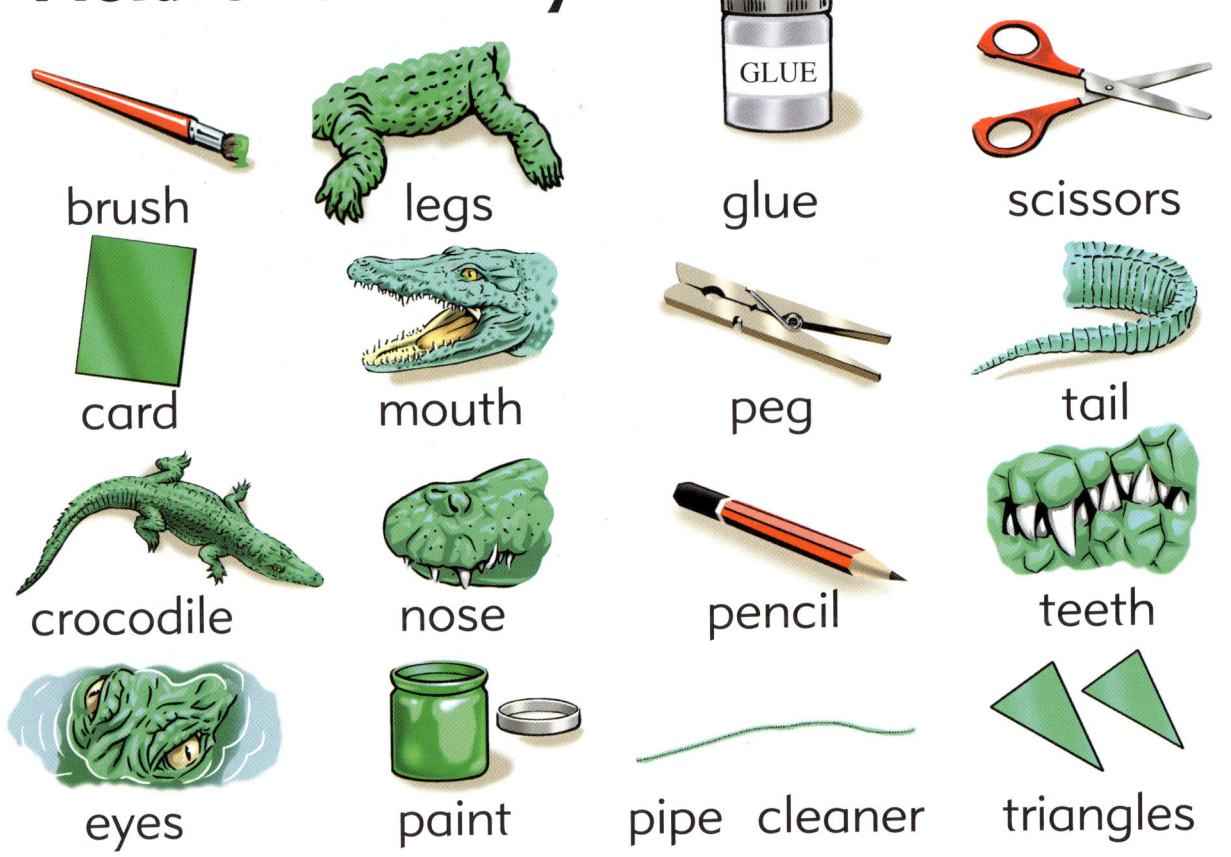